Jobs
That Make a Difference

Pamela Rushby

Jobs That Make a Difference

Text: Pamela Rushby
Publishers: Tania Mazzeo and Eliza Webb
Series consultant: Amanda Sutera
  Hands on Heads Consulting
Editor: Sarah Layton
Project editor: Annabel Smith
Designer: Leigh Ashforth
Project designer: Danielle Maccarone
Illustrations: Anna Lindsay
Permissions researcher: Liz McShane
Production controller: Renee Tome

Acknowledgements
We would like to thank the following for permission to reproduce
copyright material:

Front cover, p. 21: iStock.com/FatCamera; pp. 1, 20 (inset): AAP
Image/Cover Images; pp. 4 (top), 6, 7, 9, back cover (top left): Alamy Stock
Photo/Marmaduke St. John; pp. 4 (second from top), 10, 11, 13: iStock.
com/ RECVISUAL, back cover (bottom left); pp. 4 (second from bottom),
14, 15, 17, back cover (top right): Shutterstock.com/Pressmaster; pp. 4
(bottom), 18, 19, 20: AAP Image/© EPA Barbara Walton; p. 5: Shutterstock.
com/Kzenon; p. 8 (left): iStock.com/Kyle Reynolds, (right): Alamy Stock
Photo/Christian Müller; p. 12 (top): iStock.com/FG Trade, (bottom): iStock.
com/fotosipsak; p. 16: Shutterstock.com/Alexey Androsov.

Every effort has been made to trace and acknowledge copyright.
However, if any infringement has occurred, the publishers tender their
apologies and invite the copyright holders to contact them.

NovaStar

Text © 2024 Cengage Learning Australia Pty Limited
Illustrations © 2024 Cengage Learning Australia Pty Limited

Copyright Notice
This Work is copyright. No part of this Work may be reproduced, stored in a retrieval system,
or transmitted in any form or by any means without prior written permission of the
Publisher. Except as permitted under the *Copyright Act 1968*, for example any fair dealing for
the purposes of private study, research, criticism or review, subject to certain limitations.
These limitations include: Restricting the copying to a maximum of one chapter or 10% of this
book, whichever is greater; Providing an appropriate notice and warning with the copies of
the Work disseminated; Taking all reasonable steps to limit access to these copies to people
authorised to receive these copies; Ensuring you hold the appropriate Licences issued by the
Copyright Agency Limited ("CAL"), supply a remuneration notice to CAL and pay any required
fees.

ISBN 978 0 17 033429 7

Cengage Learning Australia
Level 5, 80 Dorcas Street
Southbank VIC 3006 Australia
Phone: 1300 790 853
Email: aust.nelsonprimary@cengage.com

For learning solutions, visit **cengage.com.au**

Printed in China by 1010 Printing International Ltd
1 2 3 4 5 6 7 28 27 26 25 24

*Nelson acknowledges the Traditional Owners and Custodians
of the lands of all First Nations Peoples. We pay respect
to Elders past and present, and extend that respect to
all First Nations Peoples today.*

Contents

Caring Jobs

Ben and his dog, Buddy, are visiting children in hospital.

Ben and Buddy

Carla is teaching Harry ways to do everyday tasks at home.

Carla

Sam is helping a boy to make friends in his new school.

Sam

Rose is looking after a tiny wallaby joey.

Rose

These people are doing very different jobs, but their jobs are alike in one important way. They are all doing caring, or helping, work.

People with caring jobs work in hospitals, health centres and schools. Some even work in their own homes.

Their jobs involve helping others to get better from illnesses, learn new skills and **cope** with difficult times. They also help animals that need looking after.

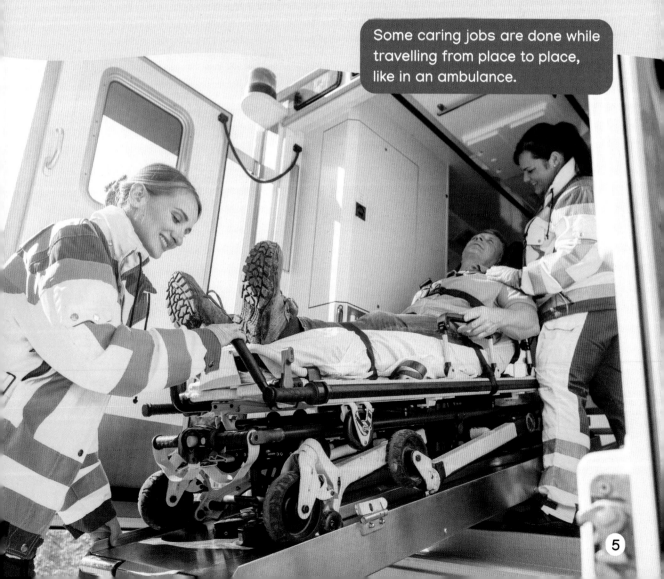

Some caring jobs are done while travelling from place to place, like in an ambulance.

Helping Children in Hospitals

It's always a special day in a children's hospital when Ben and Buddy come to visit. Ben is a trained **pet therapist** who brings his dog, Buddy, to hospitals to spend time with sick children. Ben says Buddy offers children a doggy smile, a floppy ear to talk to and a soft paw to shake. But Buddy does a lot more than that.

Ben

Buddy

Ben volunteers as a pet therapist with his dog, Buddy.

Doctors believe that visits from a friendly pet can help children in hospital to feel happy. This can lower **stress** in a young patient, helping them to feel less lonely and get better quicker.

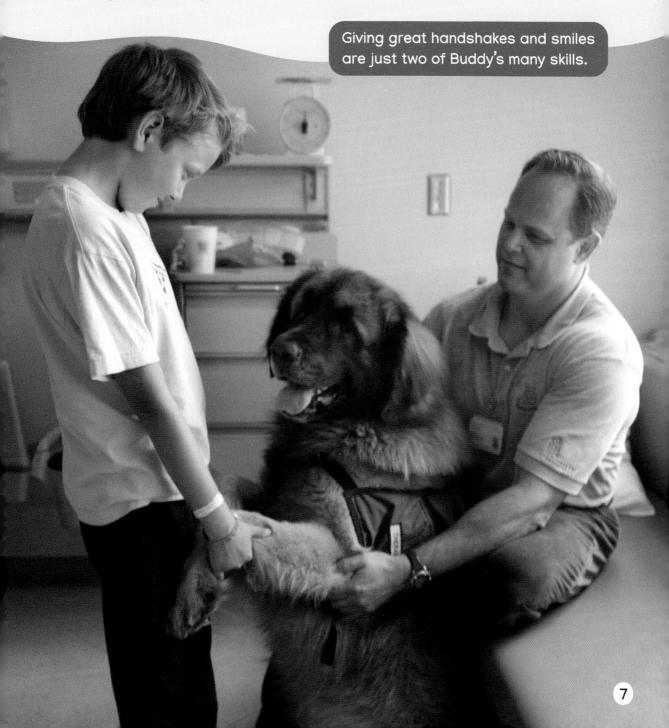

Giving great handshakes and smiles are just two of Buddy's many skills.

Ben and Buddy had to do lots of training together before they could visit a hospital. Part of the training included making sure that Buddy would stay calm when he was around lots of different people. Not every dog is suitable to be a hospital visitor, but Buddy is just right. He is gentle and loves playing with children.

Buddy did lots of training to get ready for hospital visits.

Even very little children like to see Ben and Buddy.

Ben and Buddy like to play games with the young patients they visit. This encourages children to move around and play together. In one game, the children hide balls for Buddy to find.

Ben says that sometimes children who won't speak to anyone else will talk to Buddy. Everyone at the hospital smiles and enjoys themselves when Buddy comes to visit.

Helping People Help Themselves

Putting your shoes on is something simple most people do every day. But for some people, it can be very hard.

Carla is an **occupational therapist**. Today, she has an appointment with Harry. Harry has **juvenile arthritis**. It makes his fingers twisted and hard to bend. Part of Carla's job is to find ways to make it easier for people like Harry to do everyday tasks.

Carla does exercises with Harry to help his fingers get stronger.

Carla teaches her patients ways of doing things for themselves – like eating, holding a pencil and getting dressed. This allows them to be more **independent**.

Harry can practise moving his hands with Carla's equipment.

Carla might teach some people to use special **aids** that help them move around independently, such as a wheelchair or **splints**. Other aids might be tools that make it easier to open jars or turn on taps.

Carla teaches people how to move around better in their wheelchairs.

Carla helps other people learn how to manage their **emotions** – for example, by teaching them ways of remaining calm in upsetting situations. This helps them to get along better with others.

Children can use pictures to let Carla know how they are feeling.

Harry is learning how to put on his shoes by himself.
He is also learning how to pick up small objects.
Carla creates activities that help Harry with the use
of his hands so he can become more confident.

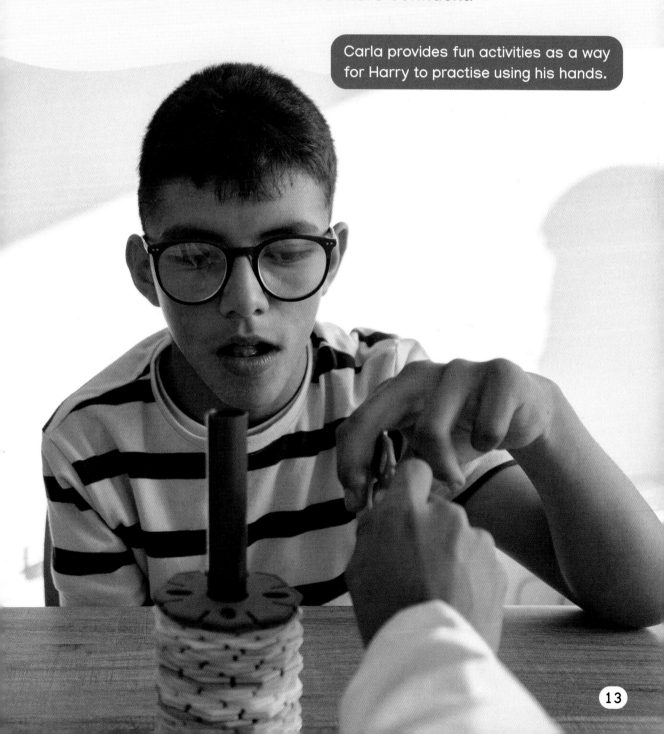

Carla provides fun activities as a way
for Harry to practise using his hands.

Helping Students in Schools

Sam is a school **counsellor**. A counsellor is someone students can go to when they need support with problems they are experiencing at school or at home.

Sam is a good listener. He hears about all kinds of problems as part of his job. Students might be upset because they're having difficulties with schoolwork. Perhaps a student has had an argument with a friend and doesn't know how to solve the problem. There could be a family issue – for example, a divorce or the loss of a grandparent. Sam has been trained to know what to say and how to help.

Sam helps students with any worries they might have at school.

Sometimes, Sam speaks to whole classes and gives lessons on things such as building **social skills** or stopping bullying. Sometimes, he works with small groups of students who all have the same problem. These students realise they're not alone when they hear each other's stories.

Sam speaks to a group of students who are all working through the same problems.

Recently, there was a flood in the town and many homes were damaged. Sam is working with some students to help them develop ways of coping with the loss of their homes and belongings.

It can be hard to go through difficult situations alone.

Today, Sam is meeting with one student. Marcus has just started at the school. He is finding it hard to fit in with the other kids in his class. Sam talked to Marcus's teacher and found out that Marcus is interested in reading and playing basketball. Now, Sam and Marcus are thinking of activities that the whole class can take part in to get to know each other better.

Marcus feels better after talking to Sam.

Helping Wildlife

Rose is a wildlife carer. These are people who volunteer to look after sick, injured and **orphaned** wildlife. They care for the animals in their own homes.

Wildlife carers might work with mammals, birds or reptiles. All of these animals need different kinds of care, so wildlife carers have to learn how to look after different **species**. Carers also need to have a **permit** to keep wildlife in their homes.

Rose cares for a baby wombat.

Sick and injured wildlife are not pets. They must be looked after until they are well and then returned to their natural habitats.

Rose is caring for a tiny wallaby joey whose mother was hit by a car and killed. The joey needs to be fed every few hours – day and night – so Rose does not get much sleep. The joey's bedding has to be changed every day. It needs a special pouch to snuggle into. Rose buys the joey's food and any medicine it needs.

Rose makes cosy sacks that feel just like a pouch to the baby wallaby.

Rose hopes the joey will grow up strong and healthy, and will be able to return to the wild. She knows it might take up to a year before the joey is ready to be released.

A wallaby joey is snug in a knitted pouch.

It is important for rescued wildlife to go back to live in the wild.

Making a Difference

People who work in caring jobs try to make other people's lives easier. Carers like Ben, Carla, Sam and Rose say that their jobs can be difficult, but it makes them very happy to do such important work.

When someone works in a caring job, they see the results of their work every day as the health and skills of their patients, students and animals improve. Caring workers can watch as people become more independent, healthier and happier.

Their work makes a difference.

The aim of all caring jobs is to help people live happy and healthy lives.

Baby Magpie Rescue

One very windy day, I saw something fall out of a tree near our house. I ran to pick it up. It was a nest – and it had three baby birds in it. They had hardly any feathers, and they were all squawking with their beaks wide open. I wondered if they were hungry.

Mum said she thought they were magpies. We were worried about predators, so we put the nest up as high as we could in the tree. But no adult birds came to care for the baby birds.

When night-time came, I was afraid the baby birds would be cold. And they must have been really hungry! Mum phoned the vet to ask what to do, and he sent a wildlife carer called Molly.

Molly said she'd take the baby birds home and look after them. I asked Molly if we could see them again, and Molly said we could. A week later, Mum and I visited Molly's home. Molly was a little sad. She told us the smallest baby bird had died. But the other two had new soft feathers, and they were growing bigger and stronger. Molly was feeding them a special mix of dog food, water, banana, hard-boiled egg and **vitamins**, whizzed up in a blender.

When the baby magpies are big enough to look after themselves, Molly says we can watch as she releases them into the wild.

Glossary

aids (*noun*)	things that give someone support or assistance
cope (*verb*)	to manage something difficult
counsellor (*noun*)	someone who gives advice and support
emotions (*noun*)	strong feelings
independent (*adjective*)	able to do things without help
juvenile arthritis (*noun*)	a disease of the joints in children
occupational therapist (*noun*)	a person who helps people to do everyday tasks and live independently
orphaned (*adjective*)	without parents
permit (*noun*)	special written permission allowing somebody to do something
pet therapist (*noun*)	a person who works with a trained animal to treat physical or mental health
social skills (*noun*)	qualities that let you talk easily with others
species (*noun*)	types of animals
splints (*noun*)	equipment that keeps a body part, such as a broken bone, from moving around
stress (*noun*)	a strong feeling of worry
vitamins (*noun*)	things found in food that are needed for health

Index